Newlyweds

NEWLYWEDS

Paul Hansen

PUBLISHING HOUSE
ST. LOUIS   LONDON

Concordia Publishing House, St. Louis, Missouri
Concordia Publishing House Ltd., London E. C. 1
Copyright © 1972 Concordia Publishing House
ISBN 0-570-06762-6

MANUFACTURED IN THE UNITED STATES OF AMERICA

CONTENTS

PROLOG

The first day of married life. A lot of us remember it. Some of you are looking forward to it. This little book is an effort to describe it.

The description is in story form. Maybe it will seem a little more real that way. I have tried to make it true to life. The language may sound shocking to some and square to others. I only hope it gets the point across. To those who are shocked, let me say that preachers are not often schooled in the delicate use of language. I apologize for being so blunt. To those who are bored, let me say that preachers don't get around enough to keep from being square. For those who can't make any sense at all out of any of the narrative, there is a little summary at the end of each chapter. Perhaps that's all there should have been to the book anyway. Time will tell.

CHAPTER 1

"Is This for Real?"

Mary got up to use the bathroom. Through the thin drapes she could see that it was getting light outside. She wondered drowsily if anyone had been able to look in the night before when they had the lights on.

She closed the bathroom door. Was that the thing to do when you were just married? Maybe the door should be left open. Should newlyweds have privacy? She remembered something she read in the book the pastor had given them when they were counseling before marriage. "There should be no shame in marriage." Did this refer to the bathroom or just to the bedroom? She vaguely recalled that there should be a difference. Well, anyway the door was shut. Mary was too much a creature of habit. And besides, she didn't want to disturb her sleeping lover. Those motel toilets made a lot of noise.

Back in bed, Mary found it hard to sleep. "So this is what it's like to be married," she kept thinking over and over. There was the faintest trace of a snore from the big, naked body in bed with her. It wasn't enough to keep her awake; just enough to irritate her a little by the sound sleep it suggested. Well, she had been told that sex exhausted men much more than it did women. But was that what bothered her? There was something else.

This was their first night together, and Joe had taken it so casually. Not that he wasn't passionate and overpowering in his lovemaking. But he seemed so self-assured and so wise and so thorough. And then he had dropped off to sleep as though nights like this had come and gone before. Maybe they had. She had never asked, come to think of it. But then he had never asked her either. She had told him that a physician had dilated the hymen to make their first intercourse easier. He hadn't questioned her—almost as though he didn't care. She wondered if men really cared whether or not they married a virgin. She had read somewhere that very few men were virgins at marriage anymore, and very few expected their wives to be virgins. Joe had tried things a few times when they were together, but she had been able to convince him that they should wait. She wondered if they could have held out for marriage if Joe had not been away for two whole years in the service. Well, she might be different, but saving herself for marriage still seemed like the right thing to do. With these drowsy thoughts Mary fell sound asleep again.

When Joe woke up, the bright light of day was obvious through the thin drapes. He wondered what time it was. His watch was on the dresser, too far away to reach. What difference did it make anyway? This was a honeymoon. Who cared about time or schedules?

Joe glanced at the sleeping form beside him. She was beautiful, he mused. No doubt about that. Her being nominated for the May festival queen at high school had first attracted his attention to her. "But she's no beauty now," he found himself thinking with a smile. "Those awful rollers! How could anyone sleep with them?" And she had insisted, late as it was when they had finished their lovemaking, that she still had to put up her hair. He had fallen asleep long before she finished. What did that mean? Was she more concerned about her appearance than about their marriage? They could have made love again, maybe. Did she care more about how she looked in public than how she looked to her husband? Of course the curlers didn't mean anything. No husband would want his wife to let herself go. He would want her to be beautiful when they were out in public; and if that meant having rollers in her hair every night, well, that's the way it would have to be.

Joe took another look at the woman in bed with him. This was something he had dreamed about more times than he could remember, this first night of marriage. He had not only dreamed either. He had pictured all the details almost as far back as he could remember. Sometimes he had worried about his thoughts. There was that Bible verse about "looking at a woman to lust after her" being the same as having her. A good youth counselor had straightened him out on that one. "Lust," he had said, "didn't mean wanting a woman. It meant wanting the wrong woman, one who belonged to someone else." That had helped a great deal.

But then there were those times when desire got out of hand. There was that girl in high school named Amy. Joe had never liked the name since. They had been in the back seat of Fred's car, and Fred and his girl had gone for a walk and left them all alone. It all looked so planned, and before Joe knew it, Amy had let him go "all the way." He never saw her again he was so ashamed. Fred kidded him about it for months. That was the first time, but Joe hated to think of the times since then, when it all seemed so natural, because everybody did it. Two years of military service may have been good in some ways, but they left their mark on a guy. Girls were so available, especially overseas. He had never gotten any diseases, thank God, but he had worried that maybe he had ruined his chances of happiness in marriage. It had helped a lot when the pastor had said that there was good evidence to show that marriages could be just as happy even when there had been previous sex experiences. The pastor had also reminded him that everything was forgiven by God because Christ had died for sin.

There had been Holy Communion at the wedding too. That should have made things right with God. And Mary? Joe had decided long ago that he would never tell his wife about any sex experiences. He had read somewhere that this only caused a wife to be unhappy and didn't do any good. He didn't quite know, though, what he would do if she asked. He hoped she never would.

Mary turned in her sleep and snuggled up a little closer. Joe felt himself cringe a little. He couldn't take much of that without being excited all over again. But she ought to sleep a little longer. She had been up late. After all, there were years ahead of them. Lots of time for making love!

Come to think of it, this was one thing that had made Joe hesitate about asking Mary to set the wedding date. What would it be like to quit making passes at the cute gals in the classroom, now that he had just started college under the GI Bill? What would it be like to live in the same house and eat the same food and sleep in the same bed and use the same bathroom and look at the same body for "ten thousand days," as one fellow put it? That had almost made him change his mind about the whole thing. Dad had sort of set him straight on that. "There isn't a man or woman who walks down the aisle to the altar who doesn't wonder with every step whether or not this is a smart move." Well, Dad and Mom had been married for nearly 25 years now. Being mixed up at first hadn't hurt them any. Maybe you get used to it after a while — this being tied down so permanently. Anyway, there was no dreaming about it anymore. "This is for real, man!" Joe found himself saying.

"If this is for real, why don't I do something about it?" Joe pressed his body close to the sleeping form beside him. But he stopped abruptly. His hand felt the stubble on his chin. His mouth tasted like leftover fish. "Maybe I'd better 'pretty up' a bit too," he admitted. "I'm hardly the kind of Prince Charming that should arouse a Sleeping Beauty."

12

Besides, he urgently needed the bathroom. Joe eased himself out of bed without waking Mary. Thoughtlessly he left the bathroom door ajar. His bowel movements were noisy and odorous. And the humming of the electric razor seemed to set the whole room in motion.

Mary awoke with a start. For a minute she was back at home, her father was shaving, and her mother was about to call for the third time. But no, the noise of the razor was too loud, and those bathroom odors—they all but nauseated her. Now she knew what the little book had meant by "bathroom privacy" as compared with bedroom "intimacy." It had nothing to do with hang-ups about sex. (Goodness knows, she had enough of those!) This was just plain consideration—like wearing deodorant or brushing your teeth in the morning before a kiss. Apparently Joe had forgotten what the little book said—or he hadn't read it or didn't care. Could she find it in herself to tell him? How would she put it? She didn't like to think of so many years of married life filled with bad odors. Well, she would get around to mentioning it sometime. Or if she didn't, the marriage vow did say something about "for worse" as well as "for better." There were some things married people had to adjust to, no matter how unpleasant. After all, Joe's family had just moved to the city when he was in his teens, and people got used to lots of things out in the country that city people couldn't stand. Anyway, she was glad he was thoughtful enough to shave and clean up.

Mary slipped quietly out of bed. What should she put on for this, their first day of married life? There was an old song that said something about "the first day of the rest of your life." That sounded sort of awful. "If this is the beginning of the rest of our lives, we ought to start things out just right," Mary found herself thinking. And all at once there came to mind those shocking words spoken a few days ago by one of the girls down at the office. "Of course if it doesn't work out, Dear, divorces are pretty easy to get these days." Now why should she think of that? How horrible! And on the first morning of their married life! Mary wondered if other people had such thoughts. Well, they just wouldn't do, not for her anyway. After all, she had been brought up as a good Christian girl, and she had learned almost from her first days in Sunday school how wrong it was to break a marriage. It was just that the permanence of the thing almost made her choke once she really thought of what she had done. "But if a thing is wonderful, why shouldn't it be permanent?" she thought. "God wouldn't have made marriages permanent if they were that hard to live with. So let's get back to digging in the suitcase and finding the right thing to wear."

"Say, what's my Sleeping Beauty doing out of bed?" Joe stood there in the bathroom door still dripping from the shower. Seeing him naked in the bold light of day was something of a shock. Mary found herself wondering why he didn't have the heavy growth of hair on his chest some other men had. Wasn't he as much of a man? And that little paunch that was starting to form around his middle! Those last months in the service must have been a little too easy. Now why should those thoughts cross her mind? Was she just being critical, subconsciously resenting her marriage?

"I wouldn't talk, Honey," Mary replied gaily. "I saw you out cold when I got up a lot earlier. So I went back to bed to keep you company."

"That's all I wanted to know." And Joe bounded out of the bathroom. "Let's keep each other company. I don't know why girls like you ever wear anything. You're so much more beautiful without. I'm glad I checked you over carefully before making any promises. None of these falsies and tight girdles for me. I want my girl just the way God made her. And that's you, Baby." The soft mattress cushioned the fall as they dropped backward onto the bed. All of a sudden marriage was wonderful again, and all the doubts and misgivings of "the morning after" were forgotten in the closeness of being just husband and wife. Somewhere a voice was saying: "They are no longer two but one."

SOTTO VOCE

In case you didn't catch the symptoms, this chapter describes "morning after" sickness. You probably noticed the "Is this what I married?" syndrome and the "What have I done now?" complex. These questions are the two most serious threats to married life in its earliest stages. (Later on we know the answers.)

There is no sure remedy for either ailment, but there are some pain-relievers. In the first case, as you may have noticed from Mary and Joe's experiences, just plain, ordinary politeness and personal cleanliness can go a long way. This applies especially to sexual functions but to other living habits as well. Note the distinction between bedroom intimacy and bathroom privacy. Ideals are sometimes shattered by bad breath, body odors, belching, flatulence, or dirt. In some societies men and women are aroused sexually by perspiration odors. Most Americans prefer perfume.

In the case of the second ailment, time is just about the only help. After a while we get used to the idea of being tied down for good. A long engagement period can do a lot to relieve the strain after marriage, especially if the exclusiveness of the relationship is maintained. No matter what the reward, it is always painful to surrender freedom.

Did you notice Joe's thoughts about premarital intercourse? There is some evidence to indicate that more and more of our newly married young people have those same thoughts. Fortunate the young man or woman who knows about the forgiving grace of God in Christ.

Confession to a counselor or a pastor can be helpful; confession to God a great blessing; confession to a spouse a great tragedy. Love avoids as much hurt as possible. Every marriage is a union of two sinners, and one sinner is no greater than another. By God's grace marriages can be divinely happy, no matter what went before.

CHAPTER 2

"Whom God Hath Joined"

"Honey, where's the little book the pastor gave us as a wedding gift?" It was nearly eleven o'clock, and the pancreatic juices in Mary's stomach were grumbling about the neglected breakfast.

"Why do you ask about it now?" protested Joe, tucking in his shirt and zipping up his trousers. "It's probably back home with all the other wedding gifts."

"No, it isn't," said Mary with lighthearted sureness. "I know, 'cause I stuffed it into your suitcase just before we left."

"Into my suitcase? Why mine? I really didn't get to look at the book, so why would I want it?"

"Because it's something for both of us, and there wasn't any room in my purse or suitcase. Dig around and you'll find it." Mary tried to be positive without appearing to nag on the first day of their marriage.

"But why now? Can't the book wait? I'm hungry if you're not, and if we don't hurry, they won't even be serving breakfast in the coffee shop any more." Joe tried to be firm without appearing to be the "dominant male."

"Oh, Honey! Don't you remember how we both promised the pastor that we would start our marriage out right with some kind of family devotion? And the pastor was nice enough to give us a little book that has readings for the first four weeks of our married life—one for each day. Shouldn't we keep our promise and start the day with a little reading and prayer?"

If Mary had felt more convinced herself, the protest would have come out a little better and with more of a positive ring. "Is this worth making an issue over?" she found herself thinking even more as she talked. "Why does religion somehow have to get into these wonderful moments we have alone together? And why does God (or the pastor) seem to be sitting there in the corner tapping his foot and saying, 'Don't forget the devotions!'" It was her childhood training, of course. For as long as she could remember, Mary's father had gotten out the Bible in the morning, and no matter who was in a big hurry, there was the reading and the prayer before breakfast. And then there were the many sermons she had heard on the subject of family worship and the pastor's strong words when they had talked about their marriage. Mary just couldn't let the matter drop.

"Oh, all right. I know we promised." Joe was rooting around in the suitcase. "But somehow the very first day of our marriage . . . well, it ought to be some kind of holiday from everything. It ought to be just for us and nobody else."

Mary leaned over and put her arms around him as he dug into the suitcase. "You're sweet, Honey, and I love you for saying that. But you know we talked about it after that first interview with the pastor. Remember how we agreed that there would be a love triangle in our marriage right at the start, because we would include God?"

"Of course I remember. But I just didn't picture it like this, I guess. I was thinking of the mornings in our own apartment when we would get back to the old daily routine. Anyway, here's the book you wanted. I guess it is, anyway. It's still in the gift wrapping." Joe handed over the book. Mary carefully undid the ribbon and the tissue paper.

"Yes, this is it. *Whom God Hath Joined*, by David R. Mace. See, here, the readings for the first week are about the purpose of marriage, and the one for the first day is about marriage as a divine institution. It's just two pages long. It will only take a few minutes. Do you want to read it?"

Joe had always shied away from reading out loud, ever since that time in the third grade when the teacher had made him stand and read the same sentence over until he could do it correctly. He must have read the sentence a hundred times, and the class laughed and hooted at his mistakes. Finally, no matter how hard he tried to keep them back, the tears came, and he was allowed to sit down. He had never been able to read out loud without stumbling after that. But he didn't want Mary to know.

"You go ahead, Dear." Joe fumbled for some kind of explanation. "My family never had devotions the way yours did. You know how to go about it. And a girl who was on the speech team at high school can do better than a dumb old football player anytime."

"OK," Mary agreed, "but one of these days you'll have to take your turn. We can't have 'the head of the house' giving up any of his responsibilities." She began to read.

"So God created man in His own image, in the image of God created He him; male and female created He them. And God blessed them" (Gen. 1:27-28). There was a quotation from the marriage service and then excerpts from a letter by a missionary to his future wife, all of which stressed the fact that marriage is not just a personal arrangement or even a social institution, but that marriage is established by God and is lived to the full only with God as a third partner. The devotions closed with prayer. Mary had really planned to say her own prayer in her own words. The family had always done that at home. But somehow the words failed her. Suddenly she felt self-conscious and tongue-tied in the presence of one with whom she had just enjoyed such violent physical pleasure. Something in her background rose up to tell her that piety and passion didn't really belong together. The devotion ended abruptly with the printed prayer.

"Joe, do you think our marriage is divine?" Mary had closed the book but remained seated on the bed. Joe was already standing, ready to go out and eat.

"Why yes, of course. We got married in a church, didn't we? And we both belong to the same church, don't we? And when we have kids, we won't have to worry about where to get them baptized or send them to Sunday school. And besides, you look divine in that curvy sweater and those groovy slacks. What more could anybody want? Let's go eat."

"Oh, Joe," Mary protested. "You just won't take me seriously even for a minute. You know what I mean. Do you think God really brought us together and that we are doing His will by being married? After last night I feel . . . well, I feel sort of uncomfortable, like God wouldn't be a party to that sort of thing."

"For Pete's sake, Mary, let's not get into a long spiritual discussion this morning. God didn't wave any magic wand or anything like that to make us choose each other. He just let us go to school together, I guess, and decided that if we didn't have sense enough to make up our own minds, He was sorry for us. That's the way I see it. And what was wrong with what we did last night—or this morning? Isn't that what marriage is for? What would God expect?" It was easy to see that Joe was getting pretty impatient.

Mary hesitated for a moment. She knew she shouldn't carry this on any farther. And yet she wanted so much to have someone with whom she could discuss her conflicting emotions. She always knew that sex was a part of marriage, and she even remembered her religious instruction that said that "one flesh" in the Bible meant having intercourse. Maybe she had read too many books or articles in magazines. At least those that came from the church so often talked about the marriage relationship as a very spiritual thing. It was kind of sacramental, almost the same way Holy Communion was a sacrament. Why, David Mace even said that in the devotion they had just read. There was the impression, somehow, that Christians would approach the whole matter of sex very gently and tenderly as they might go to Holy Communion, and not in a sudden burst of passion. Why, the way they had gone about lovemaking last night seemed almost like rushing up to the altar in church and wolfing a whole handful of Communion wafers and drinking a whole flagon of wine. Wouldn't that be a sacrilege? The minister had even read in the marriage service last night about husbands loving their wives "as Christ loved the church." Could Christ love the church the way Joe had made love to her? Someday she would have to find out more about all that. Right now she just prayed that theirs was really a divine marriage.

"I guess you're right, Dear," Mary said gently. "You usually are. I just want so much that our marriage should be the most perfect ever."

"Well, there won't be any marriage. If we don't get on to breakfast, we'll both be dead of starvation." Joe checked to see if he had his wallet and keys. "The way I see it," he said, trying to summarize in a lighter vein, "God is a pretty wise Father, and He knows we only learn by trying things out ourselves. He doesn't move us around the way my dad pushes buttons on that machine he operates down at the factory. He just keeps an eye on us, like the boss watches Dad, so He can help out if we goof up too bad. OK? I think God wanted us to have fun last night, and He wants us to go eat right now. So let's go."

As Mary and Joe left for the motel coffee shop, the book they had been reading still lay face up on the unmade bed. The title told their story better than human words could. *Whom God Hath Joined.*

This is the place where a preacher would like to spend a lot of time preaching. I'll try to restrain myself.

For a Christian couple, sharing spiritual life together should be as natural as breathing. Usually it isn't. The devil, human nature, our materialistic age — blame anything you want to. The important thing is to "break the ice," even before marriage if possible. Once two people have learned to read God's Word and pray together, they have a bond between them that others can only dream about. Try it and see.

One word of caution. Don't think devotions have to take up a lot of time. Five minutes with God each day is better than hours with Him "now and then." Regularity is the key word. That's keeping God in the marriage, not just inviting Him as a Guest now and then. "Where two or three are gathered in My name, there am I in the midst of them" (Matt. 18:20). You may also have noticed the reference to shared responsibility for joint worship. All members of a family should participate as much as possible.

Those comments Mary and Joe made about a divine marriage are designed to show the real meaning of "marriages made in heaven." The notion that God selects our mates is as wrong as the hope that He will send ravens to feed us the way He did for Elijah in the Bible story. All marriages are made by God, no matter what method a society uses for pairing people off. The important thing is to let God stay in the marriage. You notice how Mary felt squeamish about letting God stay in on their sexual activity. Too many "religious" people try to spiritualize their sex life or unsex their spiritual life. God made people the way they are. A lusty lovemaking sequence needs no forgiveness. God is there too with His blessing.

CHAPTER 3

"Breakfast on a Budget"

The waitress brought the menu, and Mary and Joe eyed it ravenously. This waiting until nearly noon to eat breakfast was something new to a fellow who made an eight o'clock class every morning and a girl who punched a time clock at the same hour. Somebody said that sexual exercise gave you a pretty good appetite too. Where did anyone get the notion that people very much in love lost their desire for food? That must have been an excuse someone invented for getting married without any money. It sounded good, but it just wasn't so.

While they looked over the menu, Mary and Joe could just feel the eyes of other people in the coffee shop. Surely nobody else knew that they were just married last night, but it seemed as though everyone did. Even the smile of the waitress seemed more sly than cordial. They were just imagining things, of course. There had to be other people eating breakfast at this hour.

"Are you still serving breakfast?" Joe asked the waitress when she returned for their orders.

"I'll have to find out," said the waitress with the air of a trial judge checking on a point of law. "Hey, Sam, these people still want breakfast. Is it OK?" Her voice echoed throughout the half-empty coffee shop like the bellow of an umpire announcing a change in lineup. Joe and Mary cringed. Now everyone was looking their way.

"No pancakes!" shouted Sam. "Everything else OK."

23

"You heard what he said?" asked the waitress. Her question sounded more like an order.

"That's all right. We didn't want pancakes anyway." Joe tried to speak softly and nonchalantly. He scanned the menu for something that would seem like breakfast but wouldn't sound too much like it.

"How about a nice breakfast steak?" the waitress volunteered. "Our steak-and-egg plate is the best." That sounded like a good quick solution, and Joe was hungry enough to eat two steaks.

"That will be fine for me," he said. "How about you, Mary?"

"Joe you know we can't afford that much. Our budget only allows . . ." Her voice trailed off as Joe looked at her sternly, obviously embarrassed.

"All right, then," he almost snapped. "You say what you want. It's still the steak and eggs for me."

"Oh, I guess I'll take the same," Mary conceded, sensing that she had said the wrong thing and feeling very uncomfortable about it.

"And how would you like your steak and eggs?" the waitress asked, with the patient air of one who had listened to the disagreements of newlyweds every day for the last ten years.

"Rare and over easy," Joe replied quickly, and Mary nodded agreement, though she had never had a rare steak in her life and had no idea what "over easy" meant. Anything to get rid of the waitress and to have a minute for private conversation. She thought they had agreed on a very tight budget for their honeymoon. They weren't going to be among those who returned from a long trip faced with the staggering bills of a "go then, pay now" vacation. In fact, Mary felt that they had shown exceptional maturity by all the book standards. They hadn't been afraid a thorough discussion of money and budgeting would spoil the romance of their courtship. They had even gone to the library and picked out a book on budgeting and spent many hours together poring over its pages. Mary had practically memorized the percentages allowed for each of the twelve major items. Maybe they weren't being realistic, but 15 percent was all they had put in for food, and that just wouldn't allow for many steaks, not even on the honeymoon.

"I'm sorry I embarrassed you in front of the waitress," Mary said. "I guess I just got carried away with our budget plans. We were going to be so careful and not break the rules."

"Oh, it was all my fault," Joe said apologetically. "But I figured we were putting breakfast and lunch together, so we could splurge a little bit. I know we agreed to no more than a buck-fifty for breakfasts on our trip, but if we add the two bucks for lunch, that just about makes the three-seventy-five for steak and eggs. We can skimp a little on dinner tonight, can't we?"

"Sure we can, and I'm sorry I made such a big deal out of it. I was so proud that you were willing to turn the money management over to me, and I wanted to be sure and do a good job." Mary struggled to smooth things over. The budget book they had read had been very emphatic about letting only one person handle the finances. "Budgeting should be done together," it had said, "but accounting and financial management are best handled by an individual." Joe had agreed that, because she worked with figures most of the time at the office, Mary would be the logical person to keep the records. He had confidence in her judgment, he had said, and she wanted to prove worthy of that trust.

Mary knew she was in for a battle long before they were married. Joe had always been such a good date when it came to spending money. "Come on, Honey, let's splurge a little tonight." She couldn't count the number of times she had heard those words. She knew too that a good spender on a date wasn't apt to be a good husband and provider. Joe's family had never had much to spend. It meant quite a bit to him to say, "Forget the cost." On his GI Bill and her salary as secretary-bookkeeper there wouldn't be much chance for that for a long time. Somehow she would have to learn to skimp on some things and let him be the "big spender" once in a while. All the books said that money problems were the first cause of family quarrels in American homes, and Mary was determined that money would never cause trouble in their home.

Joe was putting his hand on hers. "You're the best little bookkeeper a man ever had," he said proudly. "Don't let me undermine our financial future. I'll try to be a good boy and stick to my allowance." There might have been just a tinge of sarcasm in the tone, but there was love in his eyes, so Mary was satisfied.

The waitress had brought some orange juice. Joe looked at Mary, and Mary looked at Joe. Should they say a prayer before they started to eat? This they had both done at home, but at a restaurant—and on their honeymoon at that? Joe started to sip the orange juice. After all, they could still say a prayer when the food arrived. Mary said nothing but followed suit. She shouldn't push this devotion and prayer thing too far—at least not on the honeymoon.

"Joe," she said, trying to keep the conversation going in a pleasant vein, "speaking of money management, one of the things we'll have to remember to do just as soon as we get back is to transfer our bank accounts to one with both of our names on it. One of the girls at the office said she and her boyfriend did this several weeks before they were married so they had a joint checking account to use on their honeymoon. Made it look as though they had been married for years."

"Sounds like a good idea," Joe said. "Anything to keep from being spotted as honeymooners. But whatever you say on the bank accounts is fine with me. Just so they aren't charge accounts. A fellow at school put his name on all his girl's charge accounts because they were going to get married. Then she called the whole thing off, and he was stuck."

"Joe, how you talk! Who ever said anything about charge accounts? And it's too late now to call the whole thing off. But now that you mention it, I guess we ought to put both names on our charge accounts too. Didn't the pastor say we should never talk about 'my money' or 'your money' or 'my bills' or 'your bills,' but we should always say 'our'? Well, I guess the charge accounts should be 'ours' too."

"All I can say is that it's a good thing your folks paid for all the wedding expenses. That fancy spread, with the champagne and all, must have cost them a pretty penny. We'd be paying for that the rest of our lives. My car payments and your TV set will be about all we can handle right now."

"There you go," Mary laughed. "Already you're talking about 'my' and 'your.' It's 'our' car and 'our' TV set. I guess charge accounts aren't so bad if, as the book said, people have willpower enough to control their spending. It's going to be pretty tempting, though, to see all those furniture ads and not run down and buy something. It was nice of your folks to give us that used bedroom set, and I'm glad the kitchen things are furnished, but I guess we'll just sit on the carpet for a while in the living room."

"Well, maybe so. Let's see how things go after we've tried out our budget for a month or so. If we save a little on clothes and maybe food, we might be able to allow a little more for time payments. I should have a desk or something to study by, you know."

"Look who's talking about saving on food," Mary giggled again as Joe looked back rather impatiently toward the kitchen to see what was happening to their breakfast. "We'll find some way to make the money stretch. Just leave it to your wise financial manager."

Mary felt a kind of confidence born of a childhood that had never really wanted for anything. Not that she had been pampered, but she had learned the value of money and how to manage it. She had learned to get along on an allowance and do without if the money ran out. She knew that charge accounts meant paying later on, when the joy of buying had worn off and the interest had added to the price. She knew the dangers of spending everything the first half of the week and then having to pass up a good movie or an outing because the money was gone. This could mean not eating when you were on your own. She had been trained to save ten percent of her allowance, and she carried the habit over to her own paycheck while Joe was in service and she had been working and waiting. She also knew what it meant to give the Lord His share. It had been a tough job to convince Joe that ten percent for the Lord would bring them a lot of spiritual blessings. He had consented grudgingly, but Mary knew she would have to manage pretty carefully or there could be arguments again on that score. And she knew that she needed more than just that "feel" for management that the books said came with experience. She needed God's help in guiding their "financial frigate" through uncharted waters. With that help she knew she could do it.

The waitress came with the steaming breakfast. The fragrance of beef, hot off the broiler, and the rosy hue of lightly turned eggs embellished with the rich brown of chopped potatoes suddenly made the three-seventy-five seem like money well spent, budget or not. Mary looked at Joe, and Joe looked at Mary. Without a word Joe bowed his head: "The eyes of all look to Thee, and Thou givest them their food in due season."

SOTTO VOCE

On this chapter I really ought to pass. Preachers are notoriously poor money managers. There are three main points that this chapter tries to emphasize.

1. Young couples should carefully plan their budgets even before marriage. In fact, budget discussions are very valuable in the process of mate selection. They tell exactly what each person's value system is. The "big spender" on a date may be the poorest kind of husband material. The "classy dresser" may make a wonderful partner at the prom but drive a family bankrupt with extravagance. Budgets help give the real picture.

2. Budgets should not be straightjackets but should always be open to negotiation. However, they should not be changed without mutual participation and consent. Money arguments are usually inevitable; but they are much less explosive when the money has not yet been spent but is only being allotted.

3. Money management is different from budgeting. Of necessity, bookkeeping and accounting is best done by one person only, whether husband or wife being a matter of choice and circumstances. Flexibility is very important. The way should always be clear for either one to take over. And all accounts and property should be in both names. Nothing can drive a wedge between couples more readily than such expressions as "my account" or "my investment."

For further information on the subject of money management, see such references as *How to Make the Most of Your Money*, by Sidney Margolius (Des Moines, Iowa: Meredith Press, 1966), or the chapter on finances in a good marriage book like *Marriage*, by Robert O. Blood Jr. (New York: Free Press, 1969).

CHAPTER 4

"A Card or a Call?"

Checkout time at the motel was one o'clock. Mary and Joe hurried back from the coffee shop to get their packing done. Not that there was any hurry to be on their way. Everyone they talked to had said that honeymoons must not be rushed. None of these all-day drives for them, arriving at some exotic destination too tired even to make love.

Of course, there had been a little discussion as to just what that destination should be. A motel the first night, only a few miles from home, was almost taken for granted. But then there was the next stop. For Joe there was nothing like a quiet place to fish, somewhere beside a lake. Mary thought a lodge would be nice, with entertainment and dancing and a romantic view. Joe won, of course. The cost made the decision easy. They had settled on a cabin by the lake, one with kitchen privileges where they could enjoy the fish Joe would catch.

Mary was a little apprehensive. She had never fixed fish before. In fact, she had forgotten to ask her mother about the best way to do it. And she had so much wanted to make a good impression with that first meal of their married life. Mary thought of that as they started putting into the suitcases the few things they had taken out. Maybe she could call her mother from the motel. After all, they had only driven 25 miles. The cost of the call could not be that great. And besides, she was sure the folks would want her to call collect. It was no more than right that they should know that everything was going along beautifully. Much more appropriate than sending a card, or even dropping a note, not to mention the instructions for fixing fish that were so much needed.

"Joe," she began hesitantly, "don't you think it would be a good idea for me to give the folks a call before we leave? We aren't far away here, and tomorrow the call will be much more expensive."

"What's wrong with dropping them a postcard?" Joe put his toothbrush and razor into the suitcase and looked with amusement at the neatly folded pajamas, still where his mother had put them when she helped him pack the day before. Mothers were so naïve. Did they really think boys wore pajamas—even on a honeymoon? Maybe they just wanted to keep up the pretense carried on by their parents. Funny about sex. It was like that thing Mark Twain said about the weather—only the opposite: "Everybody does it, but nobody talks about it." Joe looked up when Mary didn't answer right away.

"Well . . . well . . ." she stammered in a way that was unusual for one who loved to talk. "I'd just like to talk to Mom. A card might not be delivered for a day or two, and I know she would like to know that we're OK."

"You mean, that *you're* OK. Now let's not start that kind of thing so early in our marriage. Don't you remember how even the pastor's premarital test picked out your parents as one of the points we had to watch in our marriage, you being the only girl and the youngest and all? Here we go calling Mother the first day after our marriage."

Joe had been worried about Mary's folks long before he had even asked her to marry him. Not that he didn't like them. They were grand people. And it didn't bother him so much either that they were a little higher on the social ladder. They were common, ordinary folks in spite of that. But Joe could see that Mary and her mother were pretty close. Mary even asked Mom about places to go on dates, something that seemed like none of her business. And Mary's father was always so ready to help with advice about finances. They might not manage so well, being newlyweds and all, but they would rather try to go it alone and make their own mistakes.

Joe didn't figure there would be any problem with his parents. They had enough worries of their own. When any of their children could go it alone, they were happy. There would be no meddling from that side of the family. You could bet on that.

"Now please, Joe, this isn't any big thing. It isn't as though I would run home to Mother for a visit or interfere with our trip or anything like that. While you're packing and checking out, I'll make a quick call, and then we'll be ready to go."

"Can't you see? It isn't the call that matters. It just bugs me to think you would worry about your mother on the biggest day of our lives. Isn't it even in the Bible somewhere, this thing about 'leaving father and mother'?"

"Hooray for you! You do remember your Bible verses when you get a little excited." Mary put her arms around his neck and kissed him warmly. Then with her hands on his cheeks and looking him squarely in the eye she added: "I've left, Honey, and I don't ever intend to go back. I'm yours 'till death do us part.' "

Joe took her wrists and pulled her hands away. "Of course you are; and I'm yours too, but somehow it's almost like you were calling up an old boyfriend to tell him you're doing all right but miss him. Right now I just can't have you loving anybody else or even thinking about anybody else. Don't you see? I remember how your dad wanted to pay for our honeymoon, and then your mom thought they could buy the living room furniture for us. They even wanted us to move into their basement apartment until the pastor told them how crazy that was. I guess those were the first really serious arguments we had, except maybe for the time you fought me off and said you wanted to be a virgin when we were married."

"Now, Joe, I didn't fight you off. We agreed, and you know it! Aren't you glad now?" She put his arms around her neck and snuggled up to him again.

"Go away, or we'll never get out of this motel in time! You're just trying to soften me up so I'll forget about the phone call. No dice! You even told the pastor yourself, when we were talking about equal rights or whatever it was, that you wanted a husband who would be boss. Well, right now I'm bossing!"

"But, honey, I feel sorry for Mom. After all, I was the last one left at home, and now she's all alone. I can quote the Bible on my side too, because we both learned about honoring father and mother."

"OK, OK — I guess we've taken care of that. Didn't we agree that for the rest of our married life we'd visit your folks at least every other weekend? At least we'll do that as long as we're in the same town. That's a lot more than we planned for my folks, so your mom and dad ought to be satisfied."

"Oh, I know you've been more than fair," said Mary, sensing that the argument was going a little too far but not knowing exactly what to do about it. "But then a girl's parents are always closer to her than a boy's parents are. My brother Bill and his wife don't come home very often, but they go to see his wife's parents just about every week. 'You don't lose a daughter; you gain a son.' Isn't that what the old saying is?"

"Didn't I say you were right about that?" Joe sounded a little more irritated than Mary had seen him for a long time. "But that doesn't mean you have to go and make a phone call on our honeymoon, does it?"

"Well, Mom and Dad have done so much for us that we owe them a little extra consideration. And besides, with the years you've got ahead in school, we'll probably need help from them again every once in a while."

Joe had been fastening the suitcases. He straightened up, and his flashing eyes and flushed face told Mary she had said too much.

"I'll be damned if we ever take any more help from your folks! I'll quit school first and go to work! Now you can just decide right now whether you want your mother or me. I'll take you back home if that's where you want to go." Joe was trembling he was so furious; and the tears came to Mary's eyes. She sat down on the bed and covered her face with her hands.

"So now you're ready to call if all off," she sobbed. "Just one little disagreement, and you don't want me anymore. I knew we would have quarrels sometimes, but I never thought we would fight like this on our honeymoon. Maybe we should drive back home and talk to the pastor."

Mary remembered that the pastor had said quite a bit about the importance of accepting counseling whenever serious disagreements came between them. He had told about couples who had come to see him after ten or fifteen years of married life about problems that had started way back on the honeymoon. Then it was usually too late to do anything. "Don't think that coming to a counselor even the first week of your marriage is a sign that your marriage is a failure," Mary remembered the pastor saying. "That is usually a sign that you are mature enough to make a success of getting along." Maybe now was the time to go for help before it was too late.

"I'm sorry, Dear." Joe was kneeling on the floor beside

her, trying to pull her hands away from her face. "I should have remembered the arguments we had before and how touchy you are about your folks and all that. I'm sorry I said what I did. I didn't mean it—really."

"But you said those awful things about taking me home to Mother and calling the whole thing off . . ." Mary continued to sob. Joe remembered too what he had heard or read somewhere about family quarrels. "Arguments are good for a marriage as long as they are constructive and don't include personal threats." If he could only control that temper of his and shut his big mouth at the right time! He should never have said anything about taking her home to mother. That was hard to forget, he knew.

"Won't you believe me when I say I'm sorry?" Joe wasn't much with words, and he dug hard for the right ones.

"Of course I believe you, Joe. It's just that I never thought the subject of breaking up our marriage would come up on the very first day. But I know you were angry, and I shouldn't have said anything about my folks helping us. I needed to recall other arguments on the topic.

Joe took a piece of tissue and wiped away her tears. "Come on, now. You had better wash those eyes so people don't know we've been fighting. And then you go ahead and make that phone call while I check out."

"Joe, I should have told you right away, I guess, but I was ashamed. The real reason I wanted to call Mom was to find out how to cook the fish for dinner tonight. I was going to get the instructions from her, and I forgot. I did so want to have you think I was a good cook!"

"Aw, Honey, I love you! I should know better than question what you want to do. And I think your mom is wonderful too. You tell her so when you call her." As the two stood clasped in a warm embrace, the room seemed to echo the ancient words, "Therefore a man [or a woman] leaves father and mother and cleaves to a mate."

35

Here I am reminded of the classic example of what the psychologists call ambivalence: "watching your mother-in-law drive over a cliff in your new Cadillac." All the old mother-in-law jokes have a tendency to put the blame for in-law problems on the bad acting of parents, most often mothers. I won't defend the possessiveness that fastens the apron strings in the first place; but there are good studies to show that the failure of young people to cut the strings is just as common a cause of in-law difficulties. You will notice that Mary has that problem. Girls (because of their training) tend to be more dependent on parents than boys. Husbands should be sympathetic in that respect. However, wives also need to understand the fierce need for independence in the average male (also due to home conditioning). The best rule: show lots of love and affection, but ask neither advice nor assistance.

The subject of family arguments shows up in this chapter too. If husband and wife never argue, one of them is obviously unnecessary. Good arguments usually produce good results. But there is a difference between "constructive" and "destructive" quarrels. The former deal with issues. The latter deal in persons. Never resort to name-calling and offensive speech to reinforce an argument. Bad language only admits defeat anyway.

Note the reference to marriage counseling. Here the old adage about "an ounce of prevention" applies. Pastors are more than happy to do "preventive counseling." Don't wait until the disease is too far gone to check. Couples who see a counselor early in their married life are not admitting failure; they are insuring success. If your pastor can't help, he will recommend a good marriage counselor. Don't just choose at random from the phone book.

CHAPTER 5

"Is Silence Golden?"

The car hummed along the highway toward Pleasant Lake. Mary and Joe sat close together as honeymooners should. The gang had properly painted the car the night before, so there were the suggestive honks from cars that went by. The afternoon was beautiful. They were driving through wooded country. Only a two-hour drive separated them from their "hideaway." What more could they want?

Mary could think of one thing. Not that Joe was using both hands for driving. That was all right. It was safer that way, especially on these narrow roads. And Mary had learned to expect what one writer called "a change of pace from courtship to marriage." When you can make love in bed and have all night to do it in, you don't need to take advantage of every minute in the car.

But Joe was more silent than usual. Oh, he had never been the really talkative sort. Mary could remember when she rattled on until Joe would pat her on the back and ask if she didn't need to breathe. He would laughingly refer to a wife as "a thing of beauty and a jaw forever." Most men were like that, she had heard. They were "strong and silent" while women were "weak and windy." But still Joe had been able to hold his own in a conversation, and it didn't seem to Mary that there had been long, awkward periods of silence when they were going together.

"A penny for your thoughts," she volunteered, struggling for something to get the conversation going.

"If that's all they're worth, I'll wait for the stock market to improve," Joe replied with a squeeze of her hand as it rested on his knee. "I guess I was just wondering how many fish I could catch for our supper tonight, now that you've got instructions for fixing them."

"Well, you know there's a little grocery store about a half mile from the lake. While I'm getting the other things for our dinner, I'll get a couple pounds of hamburger — just in case."

"How dare you question my skill as a fisherman!" Joe was smiling broadly, and Mary felt she had hit on a good topic. Fishing was one area in which Joe felt secure enough to laugh at himself. Mary had learned long ago not to kid Joe about his pronunciation or grammar. In that area he was painfully sensitive. But fishing was something else. If there were fish to be had in a lake or stream, Joe was usually the first to get his limit. He and his father had never really been close. The struggle to make a living prevented that. But on rare vacations or on weekends, fishing had been a temporary bond between them. Joe loved fishing not only as a sport but because it represented a father-son relationship he longed for but never really had.

"Why, Dear, you know I would never do such a thing." Mary leaned over and gave him a quick kiss, causing the car to swerve. "You're the best fisherman I've ever married," she said.

A smile, a hug, and there was silence again. "It is going to be hard, isn't it," she mused, "this business of communication in marriage we read so much about. Here Joe and I have known each other since high school, but we really don't have much we can talk about that we both enjoy. When he talks about his experiences in the service, I feel left out. When I talk about business college and my years at the office, he is miles away. And now he's going to college, and I won't be a part of that. Pretty soon we'll be like all the old married couples they talk about, with nothing to say to each other except something about the house or the children. I wonder what Bill would have been like, that salesman at the office who always wanted to date me when Joe was overseas. He had such a line. Never a dull moment when he was around! But cut it out, Silly. You love Joe even if he isn't the world's best conversationalist. You knew that before you married him. Just give us a few weeks to get adjusted, and we'll be talking up a storm."

Mary tried to think of how things were in her own family. She had always considered her father and mother very happily married. But now that she thought of it, she couldn't remember that they ever carried on a lot of conversations around the house. In fact, she could remember evenings when Mom would be reading a book and Dad would be poring over some papers he had brought from the office, the rest of the family, when they were home, would be watching TV, and nobody said a word all evening except maybe to ask Mom for a Coke or cup of coffee. Then why did all the experts talk about the importance of communication? Mary remembered reading a magazine article somewhere that told how studies had been made of marriages after five years, ten years, and so on, and the article said it had been proved that most marriages deteriorated with time. She remembered that one of the most important tests of this conclusion was the fact that couples talked together less and less as the years went by. She had always thought this referred to people who had been married for years and years. Here she and Joe were on the first day of their honeymoon, and already they were talking less. Was this a sign that their marriage too was doomed to deteriorate?

"What would you like to talk about?" Mary thought she would try again. "I get kind of lonesome sitting here doing nothing while you're driving."

"Want to drive awhile?" Joe was no help at all. "You can watch the road, and I can use my hands for other more interesting things."

"Oh, no you don't! Not if I'm driving. I've got to keep my mind on what I'm doing." Mary found herself blushing in spite of her efforts to be casual. She just wasn't used to it yet, this business of talking about sex and sex play in such an offhand way any time of the day. "How about just telling me how much you love me and saving the demonstrations for later on?"

"Say, what is this thing you've got about conversations? Never used to be that way when we were dating. Why, we used to park out there by the airport for hours without saying a word. You didn't worry then that I didn't talk enough. I didn't have to say, 'I love you,' over and over, just to prove it to you."

"Now, Sweetheart, you know that was different. We were just too busy kissing and all that. There wasn't any chance to talk. But we can't go through married life necking by the airport." Mary had to admit that this was what had worried her most about their relationship before they were married. So much of it had seemed to center in physical attraction. She knew she was pretty and had a good figure. And Joe had the kind of physique that made the girls exercise real self-control. It would have been the easiest thing in the world to go all the way before marriage. She had even hurried their wedding on that account. But still she wanted the attraction to be so much more than physical. She wanted the marriage to be more than a good sex match. She didn't want to be just "a good body" to Joe.

"We'll do our necking in bed now," said Joe, agreeing. "But how does that change anything? Just because we're married, do we have to spend all the rest of the time talking? You know I'm not smooth with words like some of these fellows you've dated. I like to do my lovemaking with the equipment God gave me. That's much more fun than conversations anyway. Want to drive?"

"No, Honey, you just keep on driving. It's safer that way. But I guess you're right about the conversations. I guess I'm trying too hard to make our marriage work."

"You mean it's that bad already that you really have to try?"

"Don't put it like that! I don't know where I got the idea that if two people didn't talk to each other, they must not care about each other. I guess girls are supposed to talk more than boys anyway. Maybe that's why. When we go to parties, doesn't everyone think that the more you talk the more sociable and friendly you are?"

"Well, I always thought about marriage as a way of working together." Joe's practical nature was taking over. "My dad says that men who do a lot of talking down at the plant are usually the first ones to get fired. When you're supposed to be concentrating on a job, the less you talk the better it is most of the time. I don't care much for parties anyway; and if I had to think of marriage as a life-time of trying to be the life of the party, well, I don't know . . ."

"My, I didn't know you were such a philosopher." Mary was impressed by the way Joe had figured things out. She liked his idea of marriage as a working partnership rather than a party. If you looked at it that way, the whole business of carrying on a conversation wasn't so important after all. "You mean we mostly ought to talk when we have things to say that will help us work together better?"

"Yes, I guess that's what I had in mind." Joe seemed pleased that Mary valued his opinion. Up to now he had felt pretty inferior when it came to conversations. Maybe his going to school would change that, but Mary had a year of business college, and then she had done a lot more read-ing than he had. She was always quoting some book he knew nothing about. He could talk a lot better if he felt people thought he made sense. "We just talk when we think we have something to say, but we don't have to worry when we aren't talking, and you don't have to wonder if our marriage is on the skids just because it's silent. Don't we need time to think if we are going to do some worthwhile talking?"

"OK, I'll try your idea if you'll just agree to one thing."

"What's that. No talk about sex?"

"No, Silly! I'll get used to that if you just give me time. I mean that just once in a while you say you love me whether you think it's important to say or not."

"I guess I can manage that. But you'll have to remind me if I forget. I don't think I ever told my mom or dad that I loved them in my whole lifetime, so I'm just not used to that sort of thing. But if you let me know when I forget, I'll promise to say those magic words every once in a while. Only thing is, you've got to know that I mean them a lot more often than I say them."

"Oh, Darling, I know you do, and I won't nag you about the words any more than I can help. I'll try to get used to the idea that silence can say more than words lots of times and that silences are good for a marriage too. Remember that text the pastor used last night for our wedding? He said it over so many times I think I can say it from memory. It didn't say anything about talking up a storm, it just said: 'Stand firm in one *spirit*, with one *mind* striving side by side' (Phil. 1:27). I guess we can do that without words."

SOTTO VOCE

What do you think of the conversation about conversation? This chapter touches on one of the most controversial areas of family life. Many studies of marriage adjustment have used "communication" as a valid indicator of success or failure in husband-wife relationships. Other scholars point out that the achievement of common goals is far more important than merely discussing them. You can probably tell that I am inclined to agree with the latter viewpoint, so I have had Joe and Mary reach that conclusion. We live in such a nervous age that we feel uncomfortable. We don't know how to use silences. Seems to me God made woman as a "helper fit for man," not as a "speaker tuned to him." I don't want to excuse the voiceless virility that sometimes passes for manhood. Men, as well as women, need to learn to express themselves when there is something to say. But talk for talk's sake is not communication.

CHAPTER 6

Sex Without Words

The honeymoon cottage had to be close now. Mary and Joe had been driving for about two hours, and the map showed only a hundred miles. Of course, one didn't drive too fast on these narrow roads—especially on a honeymoon. There was no reason to hurry. It was still the middle of the afternoon, plenty of time to get settled in the cottage—and for Joe to get out and catch those fish for their evening meal.

Silence had settled down again over the honeymoon car, and Mary's thoughts went back to the night before and ahead to what would be their second night together. She might just as well face it. She was not a very good sex partner for Joe. He had told her that she was a good student and would learn in no time at all. But she sensed some disappointment in his optimism. She had wanted so much to make their first night a perfect one—all of their marriage for that matter. It just hadn't worked out that way. She consoled herself by wondering if anybody's marriage ever did.

Mary had planned that first night so carefully. Oh, she was worried about it. No use denying that. She had even toyed with the idea of planning the wedding so it would come right in the middle of her menstrual period. Then they would have to postpone sex for a while, and she could get a little more accustomed to being married first. A friend told her she had done that. But that would just be delaying the inevitable, and she was sure Joe would be irritated. He had fussed about those monthly periods sometimes when she had let their petting go much farther than she felt it should have.

Maybe that was part of her problem now. In high school a boy had aroused her to the point where she let him explore her whole body. She had felt so guilty about that afterward that she hadn't been able to sleep well for weeks, and she had made some excuses for not taking Holy Communion at church. She was sure she was unworthy. And then she had let Joe explore regularly. She had explained to herself that they were going to be married anyway. The guilt didn't seem so sharp anymore, but it was there, and it just made her tense up whenever the caresses got close to the "pelvic area," as her mother referred to it. She had never been able to reach a climax, or "come," as Joe described it. She had asked the doctor about it. He examined her carefully and said that nothing was wrong. She would just have to learn to relax. But how?

So Mary had planned to set the stage as dramatically as possible. Mom had helped her pick out what the store called a "nude" negligee. Mary remembered with a smile how shocked she had pretended to be at her mother's daring. There weren't any spoken instructions. Mom was too reserved for that. But the implication was that a young bride should slip into something as seductive as possible to encourage a bashful husband on that first night. That was pretty amusing; but the idea of a covering, however sheer, seemed so much more secure than unabashed nudity. Well, the negligee and "nightie" were still in the suitcase undisturbed. Maybe tonight she would have a chance to use them. Joe might be willing to put up with a little more of what he called "foolishness" now that they were "old married people."

Mary wondered if all men approached their wives in

the same way. Joe had seemed to be in such a hurry to get to the climax. Oh, they had kissed each other passionately after he carried her over the "threshold" of the motel room. Then he took off the jacket of her suit and was ready to undo her blouse when she excused herself to go to the bathroom. She turned on the water in the tub full blast for fear Joe would hear her use the toilet. And when she was through, she hesitated. Should she undress further before coming out? She should have brought her new nightclothes in with her. When Joe shouted, "Hey, aren't you about finished?" she decided to go no farther and see what happened. Joe was sitting on the bed. He suggested they undress each other. She wanted to turn out the lights first. He said he wanted to see what he had married, so she gave in. Joe didn't seem to have any trouble with the feminine hooks and snaps. Buttons, belts, and zippers defeated her nervous fingers, and Joe impatiently took over. All at once they were naked in bed, and all the dramatic planning had been forgotten.

Joe had been considerate and had kissed and fondled her for a short time. But he was anxious to get on with the act itself, and she scarcely realized what had happened before it was over. She had to admit she had been a little disappointed. She was glad, of course, that there had been no pain. That was something she had been vaguely afraid of since she first knew how babies were "made." But the doctor had asked her permission to dilate the hymen ahead of time and had assured her that there would be no discomfort at all. He was right on that point, but surely the first experience should have been more than just comfortable. She didn't really know what to expect from an orgasm. She had never experienced one that she knew of. It had always seemed wrong to her to touch her own sex organs any more than necessary. She had read that some women never did reach a climax during intercourse. Maybe she was one of those. She would probably have to accept that. It was fun, anyway, just being so intimate and so close, and she was happy to make Joe happy. Only Joe didn't want to let it go at that. He knew very well that she had not really been satisfied. He asked her to go and wash up a little, and then they would try some more.

Well, they had tried, but as Mary relived the night before, she couldn't help wondering if old guilt feelings about sex had made her less responsive than she should have been. She remembered the time some of the neighbor boys had persuaded her to undress out in the garage so they could see what a girl looked like. Her mother had come upon the scene and had been furious, reporting the incident to the boys' parents and lecturing her again and again on how sinful she had been. Once after a bath she had tried exploring her own sex organs only to have her mother slap her hands and tell her that "nice girls" didn't do that sort of thing. There were probably a lot of other things she couldn't remember, not to mention the terrible guilt she had always felt when she let a boy touch any part of her body. Even the way she and Joe had played with each other's bodies before marriage had left her feeling very unclean. Now it was hard to think that sex could suddenly be all right. Maybe a girl wasn't supposed to enjoy it, not any more than she enjoyed getting meals for her husband or doing his laundry.

Joe certainly didn't agree with that. He had shocked her by some of the ways he had attempted to arouse her passions. Joe reminded her that even the pastor had said, "No kind of sex activity is wrong when you are married as long as it is pleasing to both of you." "Surely he didn't mean anything like that," she had responded. Joe had been considerate and let the matter drop; but now Mary had second thoughts. Was she just being a prude? She and Joe would have to talk about that. Maybe she would have to talk to the pastor again or a doctor. Only there wouldn't be time before that second night in bed together.

Maybe a couple so newly married doesn't really develop ESP to any significant extent, but no psychic phenomenon was necessary to keep Joe's mind on much the same subject during the time Mary had been lost in her reverie.

Joe was worried about the impression he had made that first night. Had he been in too much of a hurry? He hadn't intended to let it all happen so fast, but he had just been too excited. He hoped he didn't have the problem the books called "premature ejaculation." He had no trouble on previous occasions, but then he had never loved other girls as he loved Mary. And then there was something about knowing you were man and wife, with everything legal and right with God too. He might be a "man of the world," but deep down inside there had always been pricks of conscience. And besides that, he had always worn a rubber condom before. A fellow couldn't be too careful about diseases, and he didn't want to get any girl pregnant. The surroundings had always been a little unpleasant too. The back seat of a car was pretty awkward, and some of those smelly places overseas had almost turned his stomach. The comfortable bed and the sweet fragrance of Mary's body had made all the difference in the world. Fellows who thought it was smart to try a girl out sexually before marrying her weren't really giving her a chance. No wonder the girls who got "tested" that way didn't usually "pass." He was really glad Mary had insisted that they wait.

The thing that troubled him most, though, was the fact that he had not been able to bring Mary to a climax that first night. Was he doing something wrong? Did Mary really love him? Before marriage they had tried petting to climax a number of times. Mary had been able to turn him on without any trouble; but he hadn't succeeded in bringing her to a climax then either. Only then he could explain her lack of response by the fact that he knew she felt guilty about the whole thing. Now they were married, and there shouldn't be any guilt at all. What else was wrong? The doctor had checked her over and said she was well equipped. There was nothing left to blame but his own bungling technique.

Joe was sure that other techniques could be tried if Mary would only agree. They would have to discuss the subject some more. What the books called "oral-genital contacts" couldn't be all that wrong. Anything was worth a try if only Mary could get over some of those old-fashioned ideas her mother had given her.

As Joe looked at Mary, sitting so close to him there in the car, he couldn't help wondering how a girl who had such a sexy figure could have such "unsexy" feelings. Nature could play tricks on a fellow that way. It really wasn't nature's fault, though. People had spoiled things, people like Mary's parents, in spite of their good intentions. Maybe that was what had happened when sin came into the world back there at the beginning. Joe remembered something about Adam and Eve being ashamed of their nakedness all of a sudden. He didn't know why girls should have gotten more than their share of shame, but it seemed as though they had. Probably their mothers had drilled it into them for fear they would get pregnant. Fathers worried some about their sons getting VD and things like that, but they didn't seem to be overly concerned. He remembered his father saying something once about "social diseases," and it took a while to figure out what that meant. A Scout leader had warned against masturbation once, but all the other boys did it, so Joe hadn't really worried. He wondered if girls got more severe warnings. He wondered, come to think of it, if girls ever masturbated. He would have to ask Mary. If they didn't, maybe that was why they had trouble reaching a climax after marriage. Maybe all they needed was practice.

No matter how you looked at it, Joe thought as he turned the car onto the little gravel road that led to their "dream cabin," human beings had made a mess of some pretty fine natural desires God had given them to start with. So now there were "sex problems," and there was the need to learn "sex adjustment." Apparently it was all pretty simple at the beginning. "They shall be one flesh," God had said (Gen. 2:24). Men and women would just have to get back to doing things God's way.

SOTTO VOCE

I hope nobody has been embarrassed by this chapter. If discussions of sex are not frank, they are failures. A young reporter once got a job with a large newspaper by showing the editor he could summarize the Ten Commandments with one word: "Don't!" Much of our sex education in the Christian era could be summarized in the same way. In recent years we have done a little better with giving sex information, but we have emphasized the biology of reproduction and the techniques of courtship. Beyond that there has been silence.

There are too many tragedies in marriage that are due to simple ignorance of sex as pleasure. I think we have a good example for plain speech if we just read what God has written in the Bible. Christians let the Oriental philosophers influence their thinking in the days right after Christ; and then we got the monastic orders, the pietists, and the Puritans. Today we have other groups whose ideas about sex are distorted. It is time we remember that "everything created by God is good" (1 Tim. 4:4). Sexual feelings were given by God for a good purpose. Sex should be taught as a way two people have for making each other happy with complete and unrestrained freedom. The only morality within the marriage bond is the law of love.

Recommended readings: *Sex,* by Kenneth L. Jones, Louis W. Shainberg, and Curtis O. Byer (New York: Harper & Row, 1969); *Sexual Responsibility in Marriage,* by Maxine Davis (Pocket Books); *Understanding Human Sexual Inadequacy,* by Fred Belliveau and Lin Richter (Bantum Books, 1970).

CHAPTER 7

Man to Man

"I'll bet you don't even remember the date of our wedding!" A woman's voice could be heard shouting from the cabin next door.

"Oh, yes I do," a man's voice shot back. "That was the day I caught that ten-pound bass." A door slammed, and Mary and Joe, who had stopped their unpacking to listen, went to the window to catch a glimpse of what sounded like a rather unusual couple. A man could be seen outside the cabin checking over his fishing gear as though ready to head for the lake.

"Going fishing?" Joe opened the cabin window and put his head out. He had hoped in a way that there would be someone with whom he could strike up a fishing friendship. Mary had never cared about fishing and insisted she never would. In fact, she wasn't much for the outdoors at all. She liked to read, and she dearly loved the movies. She could name most of the pictures of recent years and describe the plot, the leads, and the supporting casts. Joe read for profit rather than pleasure, and the theater bored him, except of course the drive-ins where there had been other interests beside the screen. He loved to hunt and fish. In fact, he loved anything in the outdoor life. They had both been worried about this at first, and they were helped a lot by the pastor's comment that recreation really didn't need to be shared at all. He had said that recreation was one of the least important areas of agreement for a successful marriage. Anyway, that was how Joe had convinced Mary that it was perfectly all right to spend their honeymoon at a lake where he could fish and she could read.

"Yes, I could use a partner," shouted the rather weather-beaten and bewhiskered fisherman as he strapped on his creel. "I've got a boat down on the lake here if you'd like to get on board."

"Just give me a minute to get ready!" Joe turned to grab the old army fatigues he had brought along as fishing clothes. "Can you unpack the rest of the things, Dear? A boat will be so much better than fishing at the edge of the lake. We'll be sure to have some fish for supper this way." And then seeing Mary's rather hurt look, he continued, "Maybe you could go over and get acquainted with Mrs. — whatever their name is. She might even give you some hints on fixing fish." An enthusiastic kiss, and he was off, to dig in the trunk of the car for his fishing gear and then for a couple of hours on the lake before dusk.

"Say, Mike, what was that thing you and Anne were saying about your wedding day back there at the cabin?" The two of them had been out on the lake now for about an hour, and Joe felt he was well enough acquainted to ask the question he had been itching to bring up. Joe already had two beauties, and Mike had just reeled out his line again after pulling in a big one, so the business of fishing was not quite as urgent as at first.

"Oh, that," and Mike let out a hearty guffaw that sent five curious fish scurrying for safer waters. "That's just an old joke we heard somewhere when we were first married, and we keep repeating it every time I go fishing. We used to have some of the damnedest arguments about my fishing. The old lady went with me at first, but I was always having to bait her hook, and she was screaming like hell and scaring the fish. She never did catch anything anyway, so finally she started staying at home and griping when I came back at night. We almost busted up over this whole thing until we saw how stupid we were. She agreed to shut her trap about my fishing if I would go dancing with her over at the lodge a couple of times a week. That's where we heard that joke by the way, one of the first times we went over there. So now she yells it at me whenever I take off, and I holler back. Sort of takes the edge off, because she still think she's neglected. We don't have any kids, you know."

"Say, that sounds like a good idea. You know, having a sort of private joke and all. Mary and I will have to try that."

"As an old married man to a beginner, let me tell you that one thing it takes to stay married is a good old belly laugh once in a while. That beats all this adjustin' and communicatin' and counselin' they talk about. Anne goes to some of her ladies club shindigs, and she'll come home with some pretty good ones. For a dame she can handle jokes pretty good. I bring some home from the shop too. At first they didn't go over so big. Anne thought she was supposed to be insulted or something. But she can take 'em like a man now, and we really have a gas trying to top each other. I'd bring home *Playboy* magazine and catch all kinds of hell at first. Now we read it together, and we both laugh. When I hear from the guys at the office how some of their women nag and crab, I wouldn't trade my old lady for anyone. Take it from me."

"Sounds like you've got a good thing going," Joe responded, not quite knowing what comment to make. "I didn't mean to turn you on like that. Maybe we ought to cool the conversation for a bit and see if we get any more bites." Mike nodded, and the advice stopped for a while, but Joe didn't stop thinking. He had heard a lot about this sense of humor in marriage, but he had never thought about telling jokes and all. He wasn't quite sure what Mary, with her background, would think of the gutter-type humor. Maybe it would help, though, to break down some of that reserve. And *Playboy* magazine. Would they take that out of their education budget? Or would it be recreation? He doubted that Mary would sit still for that.

Joe was wondering too what the pastor might have said to some of Mike's remarks. Somehow it had never occurred to him to ask about the kind of humor married people could share. Could he tell Mary the jokes he had heard in service—those he could remember? Did she have some favorites she had heard from the girls and was afraid to tell him? Could telling jokes, no matter what kind, be any more wrong for married people than all the intimate things they did together as husband and wife? Years ago, Joe seemed to remember, the ministers used to talk more about how bad it was to tell "dirty jokes" and all. He couldn't remember hearing much about that subject lately. Maybe times were changing. Or maybe the idea was that you shouldn't share the sexy kind of humor anywhere else, just like you didn't share your sex anywhere else, but it was all right with your mate. He would have to find out more about the humor bit. He remembered that even in the service those men got along best who could crack a joke when the going was roughest—even a coarse, vulgar joke—and get everyone around them laughing instead of cursing. As he understood it, the going in marriage could get pretty rough too. A sense of humor could be a big help.

Joe's reverie was interrupted by a tug on his line. "Hey," he shouted, "feels like I've got a big one!" With the skill of long experience, he set the hook, reeled the line in a little, then played it out a little, slowly and surely bringing the fish toward the boat.

"Nice job, there, fellow!" was Mike's comment. "You really know how to handle a fish. Now if you can just be as good at handling a wife, this marriage of yours is going to go all right."

Joe was too intent on bringing in the fish to comment at the moment. But when the big one was finally landed and flopping there in the boat, he asked: "What was all that you had to say about 'reeling in' a wife?"

"I didn't exactly call it 'reeling,' but that's as good a word as any. What I meant was that you've got to learn how to handle a woman if you want to get along. If you don't, she'll get away, just like that fish could have tore loose from a guy that didn't know how to bring it in. You can give a woman a little freedom but not too much. When she starts to run wild, you just tug on that old line again. Always keep control, I say. Things are changing in this old world. Women want more and more of them 'civil rights' they talk about. My old man never had any trouble at our house. What he said was law, and you'd better believe it. He wasn't mean or anything like that, but he knew how to run the show. The young husbands I see around these days don't know which end is up. Let me tell you, a good woman likes a man who can keep her under control."

If Joe hadn't been so busy taking care of his catch, he might have interrupted sooner. "Come on now. I won't buy that," he objected. "I know that's the way men used to handle their wives, the old double standard and all that. But things are different now. Marriage is pretty much a fifty-fifty deal."

"Well, you try it your way, but don't say I didn't warn you. All this talk about fifty-fifty marriages! The men don't want it that way, and the women don't want it that way either. Take it from someone who knows. Women are just built different, and I don't mean what you think either. Men figure you out. Women feel you out. A man will battle his way out of trouble; a woman will just bawl her way out. Women don't have the brains men have, and they don't have the muscles either. That's why they have to be a lot sneakier. They'll sweet-talk you out of anything if you're not careful. 'Give a woman an inch, and she thinks she's a ruler,' I always say. They'll take advantage of you if you'll let them, but they respect you a lot more if you don't let them get away with it. They want to know who's boss. Even when it comes to making love, a man has to do the pushing; a woman can just lie and take it. A man knows just what he wants from a woman. You've got to play around and say a lot of sweet things to a woman before she gets hot. You can't tell me there's any fifty-fifty going to work between me and my old lady."

The language may have been different, but Joe had read somewhere many of the very things Mike was saying. But Mike's coarse way of putting things made them sound much more prejudiced than they had sounded in the polished language he had read. This whole business about males and females being so different that you had to spend your married life trying to figure each other out! It sounded like men had invented a lot of that to keep from sharing their lives with women. Maybe that's what was wrong with so many marriages. Too many men and women, like Mike and Anne, kept looking for the differences between them instead of finding ways in which they were alike. Joe knew he had a lot to learn yet, but he was sure (though he wouldn't often admit it to her) that Mary had as good a brain as he, probably a lot better. She might not have the same muscles; but she had every bit as much nerve and could make a pretty good leader. She did feel a little different about sex at the moment, but that was due to the way her parents had taught her, not to the way she was "built," as Mike put it. At least Joe would like to try this thing called equality.

It was getting close to suppertime, and as the two headed for the shore, Joe said to Mike: "I'm going to be thinking about some of the things you told me today, and I'll tell Mary about them too. I really appreciate the man-to-man talk. I guess the point of the whole thing is that it takes a while to learn to understand another person, woman or man." Though he didn't realize it, Joe was reflecting the important marriage rule laid down by St. Peter years before: "Husbands, live considerately with your wives." (1 Peter 3:7)

SOTTO VOCE

Were you surprised by the discussion of "dirty jokes"? Someone once sent me a sexually oriented magazine, because I said I believed it might be a useful thing for husbands and wives to share in privacy. My wife and I had a few laughs from the magazine. St. Paul said, "To the pure all things are pure" (Titus 1:15). I am sure he meant that certain kinds of pornography are in the mind. To the extent that jokes and pictures stimulate sexual desire, they are harmful for those who have no acceptable outlet, but they can be helpful for those who want to make sex in marriage more delightful. It is not necessary to accept the philosophy behind a nude picture, cartoon, or sexy joke to benefit from the stimulation it may give for good-humored intimacy. The same applies to some adult movies. Let's keep our thinking straight. And, of course, a sense of humor is an invaluable asset to marriage.

I also hope you got the point of the discussion about male dominance. More on that in Chapter 9. So-called male-female differences are largely unsupported stereotypes. Differences in male-female behavior are the result of training. Neither sex has any superiority. Even New Testament advice to women is tailored to the times, not to any timeless truth. For example, advice to slaves does not make slavery acceptable to God (Titus 2:9). Both men and women were made in God's image. (Gen. 1:27)

Chapter 8

Woman to Woman

How does one dress for dinner on a honeymoon? This was the mind-shattering problem that concerned Mary at the moment. Joe would have answered, "You don't!" It might be fun to take him up on that, but the neighbors were pretty close, and the cabins weren't exactly built for privacy. The curtains looked like they had been designed by Peeping Toms. Anyway, Mary knew she was just playing mental games. She could never be that bold.

So what does one wear for the first "home-cooked" meal in a cabin by the lake? Mary's thoughts were interrupted by a knock on the door.

"I'm Anne from next door." It was the wife of Joe's fishing partner. "I was going to come over and get acquainted earlier, but I saw you take off for the store."

"Won't you come in? I'm so glad to get to know you. Joe suggested that I pay you a call to keep from being lonesome while he was fishing, but I had to get some things for dinner first."

"Did you get everything you need?" Anne came in and placed her plump proportions rather carefully on a cabin chair. "I'll be glad to share anything we have. We usually bring most of our staples along."

"Well, I'm not sure yet." Mary hesitated, not quite certain how much she should tell. Joe liked to avoid telling people they were honeymooners; but he hadn't bothered to clean the suggestive sayings off the car yet, so there was no use trying to keep the news a secret. "I hate to admit it, but this is going to be the very first meal I have ever fixed without any help at all. I used to get meals at home, but you know it isn't quite the same. Mom was always around to ask when there was any problem. So tonight Joe will find out what kind of wife he married."

"Say, why don't we eat together this evening? I'll be glad to lend a hand. I'll run over and—" Anne stopped short. "No, forget it! I don't want to intrude on your little 'love nest' the first night. Maybe we can try getting together some other time."

"Oh, no! It would be great to have company for dinner." Mary had mixed feelings, but the idea of a little help with the meal was stronger than the desire for any privacy. "And with your help maybe I can keep Joe in the dark a little longer about the domestic disaster he married."

"Now don't start that." Anne laughed. "You young brides can cook circles around us old bats. We learned the hard way. With all the stuff that's packaged and precooked and frozen these days, all a gal has to be able to do is read to be a high-class chef. Trouble with some of us is that we won't give in. We think our way is better, and all we do is make work for ourselves while the men wonder what we do all day. No, if I had it to do over, I'd do all my housework the easiest way I could. We've never had any kids, so there wasn't as much to do. But if I had taken time for a little more cuddling and not as much cooking, we'd have missed a lot of the battles we had. Maybe the way to a man's heart is through his stomach; but there's a shorter way, I always say."

Mary was interested in this point of view. One of the books she had read had pointed out that college students used to list "good cook and housekeeper" as their number-one requirement for a good wife, but that now this item was about tenth on the list and "good sexual partner" was number one, along with such things as companionship, education, intelligence, and ambition. Apparently she was hearing the same viewpoint from the school of experience. She had been so afraid that Joe would criticize if she didn't "make things from scratch." He had said something once about the additional cost of convenience foods, but he had agreed too that the saving in work and waste pretty well balanced that out. So maybe she wouldn't be so set, after all, on impressing Joe with her ability to cook "like mother did," especially when she would have to work at the office for several years yet. It would be much better, maybe, to use prepared foods or even go out for hamburgers once in a while than to be "too beat to bundle," as some of the kids put it.

"Say, you make me feel good," Mary admitted, as she dug the frozen french fries out of the grocery sack. "Now I won't feel so bad serving these things with the fish for dinner. I got some rolls, and some lettuce and tomatoes and cucumbers for a salad. Does that sound all right?"

"Looks like you've got all the fixings except the fish. Let's hope the fellows come back with something. Tell you what I'll do. I'll go get my electric skillet. Does a much better job with the fish than these old iron things they've got here in the cabins. It's a good thing we're eating with you. I don't know how you'd ever have put away all that food. You bought enough for a boarding house."

"Leave it to me," Mary had to agree. "I don't know much about this shopping business either. I only know that Joe has a pretty big appetite, and I'd rather have too much than too little."

"Well, I'll bring over a few things too, just in case that appetite is bigger than any I've seen. And how about cocktails before dinner? Do you folks drink? Mike wouldn't call it dinner without a little something to relax first."

"I'm sure Joe would be glad. I'm just a beginner. I've

tried a few sips of Joe's drink when we've gone out to eat, but I never cared enough to waste the money on one for myself."

"Well, the only time Mike and I don't have a drink when he gets home from work is when we are going out. After he's had a couple of drinks, he's ready to spend the evening at home, and there's no getting him out of the house."

"Do you go out for the evening very often?" Mary asked. This was a topic she and Joe hadn't resolved yet.

"Once or twice a week usually. I used to feel flattered that he'd rather stay with me than go out and eat or see a show, but I soon caught on that he didn't care about shows anyway, and eating at home was a lot easier for him than getting dressed to go out. These men forget that a woman who stays home and tends to her knitting isn't very excited about watching the same four walls or the same TV all evening. Might be different when you're working in an office. Don't know. I never tried that. But my advice is, 'Get the old man out of the house once or twice a week, or you'll be stir crazy before you know it.' Hold everything. I'll be right back."

Mary mused as she carefully rinsed and wiped off the cabin dishes before setting them on the table. (One could never tell how sanitary the previous guests had been.) "I suppose Anne is right about getting out of the house once in a while, even though Joe's studies and our tight budget might make that pretty difficult." She remembered having read somewhere that whenever possible couples should choose doing something in preference to doing nothing if they wanted to keep their marriage alive. "Alive" and "lively" sort of go together, was the comment. Of course there were things that could be done together at home, but the plain fact of the matter was that couples just didn't do them. It was too easy to lapse into what was called "parallel activities," both watching TV or both reading, neither one requiring couples to pay much attention to each other. She remembered David Mace's saying that while Americans restrict the term "dating" to unmarried couples, Britishers apply it also to married couples when they go out alone together without the children. "Couples," he said, "ought to continue regular dating after marriage." Well, they would just have to see if they could work that in.

"Here are all the makings," Anne said as she bustled in with a bulging paper sack. "I see you've got the table all set. Let's get the salad made, and then we'll just have to wait it out. Those fellows have got to clean their own fish. I'll fry them, but that's where I draw the line. I hope you haven't spoiled your Joe on that point."

"No, I've never really gone fishing with him. He's brought some fish over to the house a few times, and my mother has fried them, but they were always cleaned when he brought them. You mean that's the way it should be?"

"Mary, you just let me give you a little advice while you're chopping up that lettuce. Men like to run the world, and maybe that's the way the good Lord made them. At least that's what Mike tells me. I'm willing to let them have their way. It isn't worth the effort to argue about it. But running things doesn't mean running all over people, and I'm not about to let any man run over me. I don't know about your Joe, but when you're married to a man like Mike, you've got to be a little sneaky about things to get your way. Mike used to want me to go fishing with him, but I made enough noise that it scared the fish, and I told him I just couldn't stand putting worms on the hook and cleaning the fish made me sick. So now I stay home and read while he does all the fishing and brings the fish home all ready for the frying pan. He's still the boss, and I have things my way."

"I don't know if I could ever be that sly." Mary was

just about to say "dishonest," but she checked herself in time. It just didn't seem to her that fooling a husband into doing things your way was showing any respect to him as a person, or to yourself either. "I always thought marriage was one place where two people told each other everything."

"Don't you kid yourself, Dearie," Anne said with a knowing smile. "Lots of people start out thinking that's the way it is, but they soon find out different—or they don't stay married. Most people don't even start out that way. I don't know about you, but I've never told Mike about the affairs I had before we were married. I figure that's none of his business, and I wouldn't want to know about the gals he slept with. Knowing would just get us both mad. And I wish I had five dollars for every time I pretended to enjoy sex with Mike when all I wanted was to turn over and go to sleep. The guy would have left me long ago if he knew. Most married women have secrets like this. Just wait till you talk to a few others. Men don't need many secrets. They can come right out and say what they want, unless it's some floozie somewhere. That's one place where we can get them to lie about what they're doing. But most of the time it's the woman who has to bluff her way. That's the old marriage game. Men make the rules, but women learn how to play."

"That sounds kind of ugly to me," Mary commented. "I don't know if I would be willing to play the game that way. I'd still like to tell Joe just how I feel; and I hope he would do the same for me." Again Mary was thinking of all she had read about honesty in marriage and how important it was to have mutual trust. How could you cheat at the game and then enjoy winning? Of course, she did remember something about not telling one another about such things as premarital sex, but she still thought that referred only to things that had happened before marriage and not what happened after you were man and wife. Would you still have to bluff once in a while? There had been a lot said about politeness between husbands and wives, and politeness was just a form of game playing. So maybe Anne was right after all, though the way she put it sounded pretty hard.

The pastor had touched on the subject when he had said that love took precedence over all other rules in marriage. Maybe that was the secret. Even if you had to pretend sometimes, you did what showed the most love for the other person. As she saw the fellows coming up the trail to the cabin and caught a quick glimpse of herself in the mirror to be sure she looked her best, Mary remembered what the pastor had said was a pretty good rule for all wives. It was, he said, a better translation of an old verse: "Wives, adapt yourselves to your husbands." (Col. 3:18 Phillips)

SOTTO VOCE

Quite a few points have been sneaked into this chapter. I hope you didn't miss any of them.

There's the one about compulsive cooking. Some new brides want to do things the way mother did, when modern precooking and preparing can produce much better results and very little extra cost. With 40 percent of our American wives working outside the home, the savings in time are far more valuable than any savings in money when things are made from scratch. Usually the husband's complaint that "the way mother did it" tastes better is imagination. Try the blindfold test and see.

In Chapter 7 there was something about family recreation, and that point is brought up again here. There is the danger of possessiveness when couples insist on doing everything together; there is the danger of drifting apart when all recreation is separate. "Parallel activity" (like watching TV) is really separate. "Getting out of the house" for the housewife is just as important as "a minute to relax" for the working man or woman. Here there must be give-and-take. For a more complete discussion of this subject, see the fine chapter in Robert Blood's book *Marriage* (New York: Free Press, 1969). It's called, "Companionship in Leisure."

The idea of deceit or "playing games" is broached here. What do you think about it? I would like to suggest that real goodness has to come before honesty and not the reverse. If we sinners were all brutally honest, life in our world would be unbearable. How about marriage? We need honesty to a point; but "love" is still the "fulfilling of the Law." (Rom. 13:10)

CHAPTER 9

Friends or Foes?

"Well, that was quite an evening for our first one together." Joe was emptying the ashtrays and collecting the glasses.

"Yes, and they were quite a couple!" Mary spoke as though she were not quite sure whether she should blame Joe or praise him for the fishing friends he had found.

"She's quite a gal when she gets a few drinks in her." Joe sounded almost too appreciative. "I'll bet she gives old Mike a run for his money."

"I don't know about that 'kissing the groom' business on the night after the wedding. That sounded like just an excuse to me."

"Well, you and Mike seemed to be enjoying the game of 'kissing the bride' the night after the wedding. So I guess we're even."

"Yes, you're right. I shouldn't have said anything like that. It was just all in fun. I guess I got teed off a little at the way you eyed that 38 bust of hers. I can't help it if I'm just a little 32. You always thought my body was beautiful before." Mary was apologetic and anxious at the same time.

"Aw, Honey," Joe stopped what he was doing to put his arms around her, cocktail glasses and all. "Of course I think your body is beautiful, much more beautiful than that plump partridge. But you can't blame a guy for looking, can you, especially when there didn't seem to be much under that sweat shirt. I had a couple of drinks too, and that seems to make anything look more attractive."

"Oh, I know we talked about all this before, and I promised a dozen times not be jealous, but I guess I'll just have to keep on practicing till I learn how to get over it. Repeat after me: 'I must have confidence in myself!' 'I must be loving but not possessive!' You see, I haven't forgotten the lessons. I can learn them with my head, but I can't learn them with my heart. So I goof! One of these days I'll learn that you do love me and that you do love me more than anybody else and that you will always love me no matter who comes along. Just give me time."

"OK. So we've had our lesson for tonight." Joe felt the glasses slipping from his fingers and hurried over to the sink. "Hey, weren't you the one who talked me into reading that little book about *The Art of Loving*? I never did finish it all. Kind of complicated for a nonreader like me. But I do remember something either the book or you said about the three kinds of love. The one kind a guy can have for just any sexy gal that walks down the street. No problems there unless he loses control. And then there's the kind you have for your folks and good friends and all. That's a sort of give-and-take thing. But the love you have for your wife or husband has to have these two and something else besides. I don't remember the name of it, but anyway, it had something to do with God's love and giving yourself to the other person. Am I right?"

"Of course you are. Those three kinds of love had Greek names — *eros*, *philia*, and *agape*. I know I shouldn't care if you have a little *eros* toward a girl with a great figure or if you show a little *philia* toward a good, efficient secretary, or even if you show *agape* toward our children or any poor person you want to help. Our love has all three and that's what makes it different. But why can't I act the way I tell myself I should? Didn't some prophet say that love can be lost by too much neglect but smothered by too much attention? I'll try to remember that."

"Now don't get all worried about it. I shouldn't have brought the subject up. I was really trying to find out what you thought about Anne and Mike as friends. You always told me that after we were married we should try to make new friends together and not try to keep our old bachelor buddies. Well, how are these folks for a starter? They don't live too far from us in town."

"Oh, Joe, I don't know. They're a pretty nice couple, but really we don't have much in common with them except fishing. They've been married about fifteen years; and they're pretty independent, not having any children and all. We might get all the wrong ideas about marriage from them. Believe me, Anne was pretty generous with her advice."

Joe dropped into the wooden rocker, the only thing in the cabin resembling comfort. "Yes, Mike was pretty mouthy about marriage too. I suppose everyone figures newlyweds like us need advice. The two of them ought to get over that after a while."

"I know," Mary persisted. "But I can't stand Mike's foul language either, and—"

"I was wondering when you would bring that up," Joe interrupted, as if he had wanted to mention the subject himself but felt it was hardly appropriate for a man. "I tried to cue him in when we were coming up from the lake, but I guess he just doesn't think."

"Now, Joe, you shouldn't act as if I'm the only one who cares. You don't use that kind of language yourself—or at least I hope you don't. You may let out a damn or hell once in a while when you're angry, but you don't use some of those vulgar words. I just can't get used to those." Mary was running the water in the sink, getting ready to do up the dishes. Anne had offered to stay and help, but it seemed easier to refuse rather than have company that much longer.

Joe kept rocking vigorously. "You're right, I know, but maybe we can do something for these people. They don't have any church, they said, but they seemed to respect the way we talked about ours. They even said they might go with us tomorrow morning if we went to that little church in the village. Maybe we could be good missionaries."

"We don't have to be close friends with everybody we invite to church." Mary sounded a little cross, and Joe wondered why. "I know I probably don't have the right attitude, but I just think we should pick our friends from people about our own age and from people who have something in common with both of us. You could go fishing with Mike once in a while, but that doesn't mean we have to get together as couples. Anyway, I don't much appreciate the way Mike talked about women and their place in the home and all that."

"Oh, now I get it!" Joe bounded from the rocking chair. "You're just uptight because I'm sitting here letting you do the dishes alone. I forgot. I'll admit it. I'm just not used to this housework thing. I don't think I ever saw Dad help with the dishes at home. Of course, now we have a dishwasher, and he doesn't have to. But even when we didn't . . . Maybe old Mike did get to me this afternoon without my realizing it. He kept talking about keeping women on the end of a line like you would a fish."

"See what I mean? Friends can be a pretty strong influence even before you realize it. I'm glad you woke up. I'd hate to do all these dishes alone before we go to bed."

Joe's eyes lit up. "Oh, you're thinking about bed too. Whoopee! Let's hurry with the dishes. I'll go for this fifty-fifty marriage every time if my fifty includes a lot of time in bed."

"Oh, shush!" But Mary smiled in spite of herself as she enjoyed his appreciative squeeze. "But that reminds me I've one more bone to pick with you. You and Mike were talking about this fifty-fifty business too. Don't you remember how wrong the pastor said that was? And I had read that before. One article I read said that a fifty-fifty marriage was like trying to join two 3-foot boards together to make one 6-foot board, or something like that."

"Sounds all right to me. What's wrong with that? Two threes make six, don't they?"

"Oh, I know I don't have it quite right. I guess the boards were each four feet long, or something like that, and to make them fit exactly you had to cut a foot off each one. There was something about giving up our individuality or identity or whatever it was called. If the two boards were left four feet long and overlapped, you could nail them together easily, and the joint would be much stronger. Does that make sense? Anyway, marriage is supposed to be seventy-seventy or something like that, and not fifty-fifty."

"I get what you mean. And I suppose it makes sense, if you don't care how smooth the joint is. I doubt any carpenter would do it that way."

"Well, don't be so fussy. You'd better get going on those dishes, or I'll be finished long before you and be asleep before you get to bed."

"You'd better not be, or I'll remember some of the things Mike told me about controlling a woman. I guess I know what you mean about this fifty-fifty thing. Maybe the joint isn't always so smooth when the sticks overlap, but it's strong, and that's the important thing."

"Good boy! You'll make good husband material yet. It's fun to talk, even when we don't always agree. The way you were going in the car this afternoon, I was afraid marriage had silenced you forever."

"I guess I wasn't thinking very straight. I should have talked if you wanted to. That's a part of this seventy-seventy business, isn't it?"

"Yes, and I suppose I should have kept my mouth shut if I saw you didn't feel like talking. That's part of it too. Anyway, we're never going to make things come out right if we always want to give as much as we take or take as much as we give. . . . Say, careful of those dishes. You don't have to be in that big a hurry."

"I'm ready to do a little giving and taking, aren't you? What's that old joke about marriage being a 'give and take' proposition — 'If she doesn't give you enough, take it'?"

"That's not the way it went at all. It was a mother telling her daughter, 'If *he* doesn't give you enough, take it.' You just twisted it around." Mary poured out the dishwater and was tidying up the sink. "I still think what the pastor said about 100-100 makes sense. I'll bet you weren't even listening. He said husbands should love their wives 'as Christ loved the church,' and that meant 100 percent, because He died for us. And He said wives should adapt themselves to their husbands 'as the church adapts to Christ,' which should also be 100 percent. Two six-foot boards nailed together would be strongest of all — and smooth too. How's that for being a good carpenter?"

"Bravo! You really hit it that time! Anyway, right now I'm so ready for bed that I'd agree to anything. What do you say?"

Mary and Joe didn't remember it, but in the pastor's wedding sermon there had been that verse which summed up the evening's discussion: "Through love be servants of one another." (Gal. 5:13)

SOTTO VOCE

How did you like the sneaky way I got in a little philosophical discussion of love? No preacher could write a book on marriage without getting that in somewhere.

One of the main points here is the matter of jealousy.

72

There is really no place for jealousy in a marriage. It is basically suspicion and insecurity and selfishness. The distinction between love and friendship and mere sex attraction is very important here.

The choice of friends is sometimes a serious problem for young couples. It is strongly recommended that "bachelor friends" be quietly discarded in favor of married friends the couple has made together. Married friends should have interests common to both (not just fishing for the man or movies for the woman). Christian couples also watch for the common spiritual values if they are really to relax and enjoy each other. Making friends for evangelistic purposes is something else.

The fifty-fifty discussion may give a carpenter fits. Like all illustrations, that one about the board is full of splinters, but perhaps it gets across the point when it compares the husband's love to Christ's going to the cross and the wife's cooperation to the church's complete surrender to Christ. Neither has "rights" under those conditions but only devotion.

CHAPTER 10

Blunders and Blessings

"Darling, something terrible has happened!" The concern in Mary's voice and her cool body against his warmth aroused Joe from the half stupor into which he had fallen. The day after the wedding was within minutes of midnight. The honeymooners had just completed a more satisfying sexual experience than any they had dreamed was possible. The thoughts and activities of the day, coupled with some playful but passionate preparation, had set the stage for a truly simultaneous climax. For Mary it was like starting a new life. For Joe it was the pinnacle of all that had gone before. Mary had resigned herself to weeks, even months of trying, before she would know what an orgasm meant. But she had surrendered to Joe's technique, and it had worked. Joe hadn't noticed much in the sex information the pastor had given them; but he had noticed the statement that simultaneous orgasm should be expected only rarely and that it was hardly important to good sex adjustment. He had never experienced it before and wondered if it were possible even in marriage. Now everything had happened to make both Mary and Joe feel they were just the luckiest couple on earth. Mary had gotten up to wash, and Joe, in spite of himself, was dozing off when . . .

"Hey, what's the matter? How could anything bad happen now after an evening like this? If you left your rollers back at the motel, so what? You'll still look beautiful in the morning."

"Joe, I hate to worry you, but I can't help it. I'm worried sick. Do you know what I forgot? I forgot to take my pill this morning. Now what? Do you think I'll get pregnant? Then I can't work anymore, and you can't go to school, and . . . and . . . Oh, Joe, what have I done?" There were tears in her eyes.

Joe sat up in bed. He wasn't exactly prepared for a serious discussion, but Mary's tears gave him no choice. "Don't worry, Honey. Don't let something like a little pill spoil the happiest night of our lives so far. Take another pill in the morning, and those ovaries will probably never know that you forgot one."

"Yes, but the doctor said I had to be especially careful not to forget the pill in the middle of my cycle, and that's just where I am right now. This is the worst possible time to forget."

"So you do get pregnant. We always wanted a couple of children anyway. Why not have them sooner as later? They always say the closer you are to your children in age, the better parents you can be. We'll be the best." Joe tried to appear casual, though he had been most insistent that there be no children until he could finish college. He had heard and seen too much of these tough economic struggles fellows had when they married in the service. On nothing but the GI Bill, marriage in college could even be tougher. But still they had talked about the possibility of pregnancy. When they went for their physical examinations before marriage, both of their doctors had reminded them that no kind of contraception was absolutely foolproof. The pill, his doctor had said, was from 95 to 99 percent reliable, which was pretty good. But the doctor had pointed out that couples who married without even thinking of what they would do in case pregnancy occurred were taking some pretty big chances. The doctor had even mentioned the possibility of forgetting the pill, and now it had happened.

Joe's apparent lack of concern was reassuring, but there were still those haunting thoughts of part-time jobs and daytime sitters and squalling babies and dirty diapers and a husband coming home to a dirty house and TV dinners and no place to study and quitting school and working in a factory and . . . where would it all end? Her parents would be glad to help, she knew, but Joe would rather quit school than accept that. This was just no time to get pregnant.

"Joe, do you think if I went to Dr. Potter, and I really am pregnant, he could do something to keep me from having the baby?"

Joe was a little startled at such a question. He hadn't thought about abortions since those early days at camp when a girl who slept with almost anyone had asked if he would help her pay to get rid of her baby. He had been shocked at the idea then and had told her he would have absolutely nothing to do with it. He had heard no more about it, but he had gotten into quite a discussion with some of the fellows in the barracks. They thought he had a pretty narrow view on the subject. What, after all, was the difference between using a condom to keep the sperm from reaching their goal or scraping the seed out after it was fertilized? One was no more alive than the other. He had brought in something about God giving the child a soul, but he had had to admit he didn't know much about when that happened and had given up on that approach. Anyway, the problem hadn't seemed very real before, so it hadn't really entered his mind again. Now he had to say something.

"I suppose Dr. Potter could do that; but do you think he would? Isn't there some law that says doctors can't get rid of babies unless the mother's health is in danger?"

Mary was silent for quite a while before she answered. "You're right, of course, and I don't suppose I would really want the doctor to do anything anyway if I found out I really was pregnant. It's just that we have always talked about having babies that weren't accidents but were really wanted, and I just can't bear to think of having a baby we don't want. I read something somewhere that said having unwanted babies was a crime worse than murder because it condemned children to a whole lifetime of misery. I guess that was sort of exaggerated, but it worries me."

"Oh, I'll bet our baby would be wanted no matter when he came." Joe always referred to their first child as "he," no matter when the subject came up. "We might think now that we just couldn't get along, but we'd manage somehow. Don't you remember how even the pastor told us when we went for counseling that even if we didn't plan to have a child for a few years, we should always figure out what we would do just in case? Remember how we figured it out?"

"Yes, I remember you said you had three thousand dollars in bonds from your time in service, and you could cash those if you had to; and we have your GI insurance and the policy my folks got for me. We could borrow on those. But you have almost four years of college to go."

"It won't be easy, but we can make it. Think of the couples who don't have nearly that much. Anyway, let's not worry anymore tonight. We won't starve for quite a while, even if you do have to quit working. And I won't have to quit school. And if we have a baby after such a wonderful night as this was, he'll be the most wonderful child anyone ever had. So let's go to sleep and dream about him."

"Joe, you're a darling. You're not blaming me for forgetting?"

"Of course not. It's my fault just as much as yours.

I should have reminded you. So come on. Let's go to sleep."

"Could we say a little prayer first? We could ask God to keep me from getting pregnant. Would that be the right thing to do?"

"Sure we can say a prayer. We should have done that anyway. I guess I didn't tell you before, but I've always said a prayer at night — ever since I was a kid. For a while there I used to forget a lot, or didn't really care, but when I was overseas, I started in again — regularly. It sure helps when a guy is all alone and worried. I wasn't brave enough to say any prayers out loud, but I said them. Only I guess I don't know if we should really ask God not to give us a baby. Isn't there a rule about praying, 'Not my will but Thine be done,' or something like that?"

"Darling, you're wonderful! I'm finding out more that I like about you all the time. What prayer should we say?"

"Why don't you say one, Dear? You're better with words than I am. I just know the prayers I learned as a kid, and they just don't seem right now."

"Dear heavenly Father," Mary began. They instinctively folded their hands and closed their eyes as they lay side by side there on the pillow. It seemed like the natural way to pray. "Dear heavenly Father, we thank You for being with us today and giving us so much happiness together. Forgive us whatever we have done wrong, and help us do more things that are right. Be with us also tonight and tomorrow. Don't let us have a baby unless You really think we should have one. Help Joe finish school, and help us do all the things we planned — if it is Your will. In Jesus' name. Amen." Mary found the words coming much more easily than she thought they would. Maybe this wasn't a polished prayer and all that, but she had said what she wanted to say. She hoped Joe would understand.

"That was beautiful, Mary," he was saying. "I'll let you say the prayers for us all the time."

"Now, Honey. You know we agreed to share our devotions. I never thought I could say prayers out loud—at least for the two of us. It's different in Sunday school class or places like that. There it's just the thing to do. But it's hard when you're alone together like this. I guess in one way I'm kind of glad I forgot to take the pill. Getting worried and all that helped us remember God in our marriage. Otherwise we might have gone to sleep without thinking about Him. But I still hope I don't get pregnant."

"Sure, we'll both keep praying that we can do all the things we've planned. But we won't really have to worry. Everything will work out just right. Just think of how wonderful our first day of married life has been—even with our little arguments and all."

Mary kissed him fondly and then snuggled up as they turned out the light. "I know they say you can't live on love, but sometimes I think you can come pretty close to it. Anyway, after we've done everything else we can to make our marriage work, we always know that we love each other, and that takes care of the rest."

There was a word of God that agreed with her. "The greatest of these is love." (1 Cor. 13:13)

SOTTO VOCE

This little summary could be longer than the chapter itself if I were to go into such subjects as the morality of contraception, abortion, etc. These are pretty unsettled issues among many Christian people. The trend is toward recognizing the fact that the Bible does not speak specifically to any of them.

The main point this chapter emphasizes is that couples should always be prepared for pregnancy, no matter how carefully they plan to wait for children. The failure to have an "alternate proposal" in the event of pregnancy has proved disastrous for many marriages.

Couples who can come to the close of every day with prayer to God can look forward to blessings from God for each new day.

=